50

PRESIDENTIAL LIBRARIES™

GERALD R. FORD
LIBRARY AND MUSEUM

Amy Margaret

The Rosen Publishing Group's
PowerKids Press™

New York

For Gram Johnson Baily

Acknowledgement: The author would like to thank Jim Kratsas of the Ford Museum for his invaluable assistance on this project. Special thanks also goes to Chip Emery of the Gerald R. Ford Council, Boy Scouts of America.

Published in 2004 by The Rosen Publishing Group, Inc.
29 East 21st Street, New York, NY 10010

First Edition

Editor: Joanne Riethoff
Book Design: Maria E. Melendez
Book Layout: Eric DePalo

Photo credits: Cover and title page, pp. 5, 6, 7, 8, 9, 10, 11 (bottom), 14, 15, 16, 17, 18, 22 © courtesy of Gerald R. Ford Library; pp. 4, 12 © Dirck Halstead/TimePix; p. 11 (top) courtesy of Yale University and Gerald R. Ford Library; p. 13 © Dennis Brack/Black Star/TimePix; p. 19 (top) courtesy of the U.S. Mint; p. 19 (bottom) courtesy John F. Kennedy Library; p. 20 © Jim Bourg/Reuters/TimePix; p. 21 (left) Cindy Reiman; p. 21 (right) © TimePix.

Margaret, Amy.
Gerald R. Ford Library and Museum / Amy Margaret.— 1st ed.
    p. cm. — (Presidential libraries)
Includes bibliographical references and index.
ISBN 0-8239-6270-9 (lib. bdg.)
1. Gerald R. Ford Library and Museum—Juvenile literature. 2. Ford, Gerald R., 1913– —Archives—Juvenile literature. 3. Presidents—United States—Archives—Juvenile literature. 4. Ford, Gerald R., 1913– —Museums—Michigan—Grand Rapids—Juvenile literature. 5. Ford, Gerald R., 1913– —Juvenile literature. 6. Presidents—United States—Biography—Juvenile literature. [1. Gerald R. Ford Library and Museum. 2. Ford, Gerald R., 1913–
3. Presidents.] I. Title.
E838.5.F67 M37 2003
973.925'092—dc21

2001006666

Manufactured in the United States of America

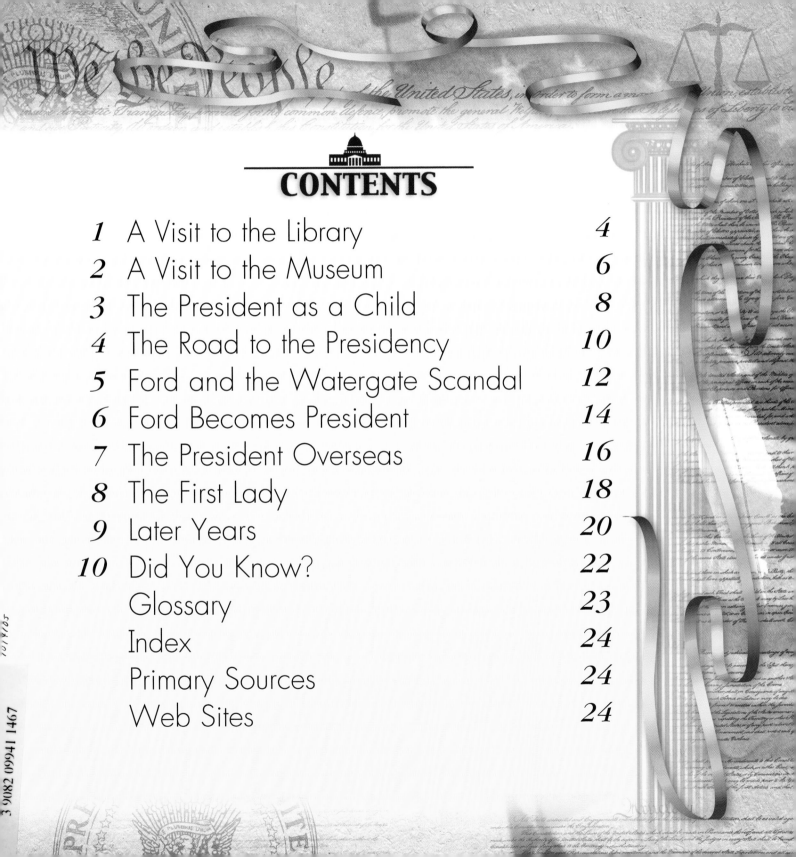

CONTENTS

A VISIT TO THE LIBRARY

Both Ford's hometown and the college he attended are very dear to him. Ford's library was built on the grounds of the University of Michigan, Ann Arbor. Ford graduated from this college in 1935. Construction of the library started in January 1979. The library opened in the spring of 1981.

The Gerald R. Ford Library and the Gerald R. Ford Museum are part of the system of 10 official presidential libraries in the United States. The libraries are run by the **National Archives and Records Administration** (NARA). Ford had his library built in Ann Arbor, Michigan, and his museum in Grand Rapids, Michigan.

In April 2000, almost 40,000 pages of material on the **Vietnam era**, which occurred in part during Ford's presidency, were made available to the public. These papers include files from the **National Security Council** staff, President Ford's own files on Vietnam, and recorded conversations between officials.

The Gerald R. Ford Library is located in Ann Arbor, Michigan. The library houses 21 million pages of letters, reports, and other historical papers on the work of Gerald Ford.

A VISIT TO THE MUSEUM

Ford was such a good football player that he was offered the chance to play for the Detroit Lions and the Green Bay Packers. Ford turned down both and found a job coaching at Yale University, where he eventually went to law school.

The Gerald R. Ford Museum is located in Grand Rapids, Michigan, 130 miles (209 km) from the library. Although Ford was born in Omaha, Nebraska, Grand Rapids is where he was raised. The museum was opened in September 1981. It averages about 110,000 visitors per year.

The building of the museum is a triangular, two-story building that cost $11 million to build. Its front entrance features a pool and a fountain. It also has a 300-foot (91-m) glass wall that gives visitors a beautiful view of the city and the Grand River.

The Ford Museum has 10 exhibit areas. The largest exhibit features Ford's early years. It includes his childhood, college years, and early political career. The most popular exhibit is the room that looks the way the Oval Office did when Ford was president.

Grand Rapids' All City First Football Team 1930

ALLAN ELLIOTT
SOUTH
QUARTER BACK

DON GUEST
CENTRAL
RIGHT END

JOHN HEINZELMAN
SOUTH
RIGHT HALF

ED KALAWART
OTTAWA
LEFT HALF

SILAS McGEE
SOUTH
LEFT END

FRANK COOK
UNION
FULL BACK

BOB KAWKA
UNION
LEFT TACKLE

TED BURGESS
UNION
LEFT GUARD

GERALD FORD
SOUTH
CENTER

JOHN VAN NORMAN
OTTAWA
RIGHT GUARD

ART BROWN
SOUTH
RIGHT TACKLE

Compliments of Heinie Martin, Sports Editor, The Herald

During high school in Grand Rapids, Michigan, Ford played center on his football team. You can see him in the center of the bottom row in this team picture taken in 1930.

THE PRESIDENT AS A CHILD

On July 14, 1913, President Ford was born Leslie Lynch King Jr. His father and mother divorced when he was two years old. His mother, Dorothy, married a man named Gerald R. Ford. They then changed Leslie's name to Gerald R. Ford Jr. Young Gerald Ford did not know about this name change until many years later. Ford had two nicknames, Jerry and Junie. He also had three half brothers with whom he grew up. Jerry's parents had three rules for him and his brothers. They were to tell the truth, to work hard, and to come to dinner on time. You can learn more about Ford's early years in the *Who Is Gerald Ford?* exhibit at the museum in Grand Rapids.

Jerry was an active youth. He played golf, baseball, and football. He also joined the Boy Scouts. At the age of 14, he became an Eagle Scout, which is the highest rank in the Boy Scouts of America. Here Jerry is shown with his troop raising a flag at Fort Michilimackinac at Mackinac Island State Park, Michigan.

This is a picture of Jerry in his high school football uniform. Jerry not only did well in sports, but also he did well with his schoolwork. He was chosen for the National Honor Society and graduated in the top 5 percent of his class.

Jerry (fifth from the right) is standing with his Eagle Scout Guard in 1929. His group used to be guides during the summer in Mackinac Island State Park, Michigan.

THE ROAD TO THE PRESIDENCY

After high school, Ford attended the University of Michigan. He studied **economics** and **political science**. After graduating Ford found a job as the freshman boxing coach and assistant football coach at Yale University. After three years, he was accepted into Yale Law School. He graduated in 1941.

After serving in the U.S. Navy, Ford entered politics in 1948. He joined the **Republican** party. He won his first election and became a representative for Michigan in **Congress**. In 1965, he was elected to be the **House minority leader**. His letters and documents from this time in Congress are housed at the Ford Library. Ford served in Congress until 1973.

When Ford was finished in Congress at the end of the day, he would go back to the office, sign letters, meet with people, and head home at around 5:30 P.M. After dinner, he prepared for the next day and read the newspapers. His working day would be about 11 hours long! The picture above was part of a special article in Junior Scholastic, about the life of a congressman.

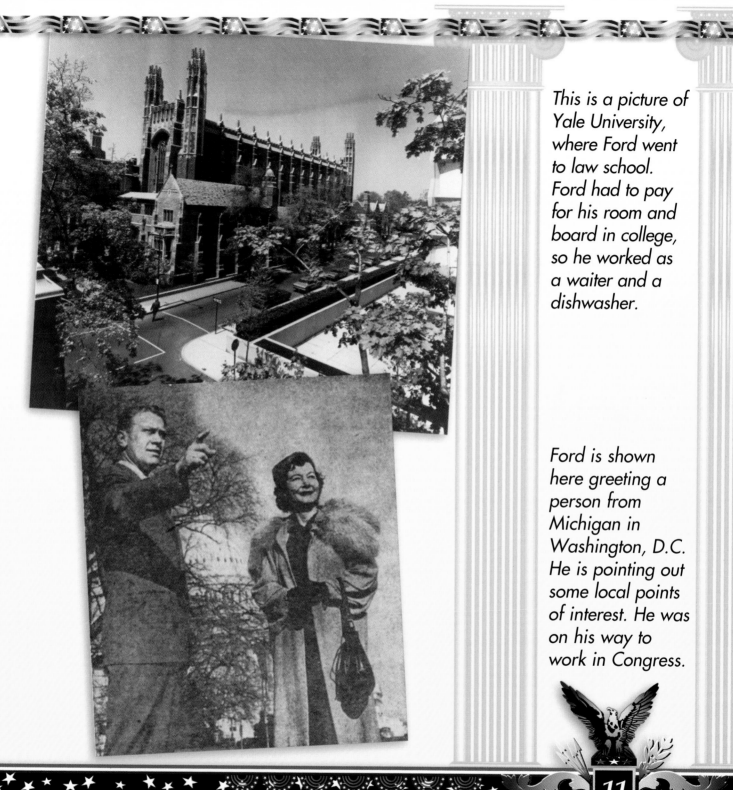

This is a picture of Yale University, where Ford went to law school. Ford had to pay for his room and board in college, so he worked as a waiter and a dishwasher.

Ford is shown here greeting a person from Michigan in Washington, D.C. He is pointing out some local points of interest. He was on his way to work in Congress.

FORD AND THE WATERGATE SCANDAL

President Nixon was allowed to pick a new vice president because of the Twenty-fifth Amendment to the Constitution. After Nixon chose Ford, the FBI did a background check on Ford. This was the most thorough check in FBI history. Ford was sworn in as vice president on December 6, 1973.

In 1972, two newspaper reporters uncovered the **Watergate Scandal**. That year five people had broken into the **Democratic** national headquarters at the Watergate hotel and office building in Washington, D.C. They were looking for secrets to the Democrats' plan to win the presidency in the next election. The burglars were connected to the Republican party. The scandal lasted for two years. On display at the Ford Museum are the actual tools used to break into the headquarters at the hotel.

During this time, Vice President Spiro Agnew **resigned** in October 1973. He was accused of accepting **bribes** and of not paying his taxes as governor of

Maryland. President Nixon selected a new vice president. The **House of Representatives** and the **Senate** had to approve his choice. President Nixon chose Ford and Congress accepted him. Ford became vice president.

This photograph shows Gerald and Betty Ford walking with Richard and Pat Nixon. President Nixon had to leave the presidency after it became known that he was involved in the Watergate Scandal.

FORD BECOMES PRESIDENT

This is Nixon's letter of resignation, which is kept at the Ford Library. Ford's pardon of Nixon angered many Americans. They didn't want Nixon to get away with any crime that he might have done. Many people believe the pardon was the main reason Ford did not win the 1976 election.

Less than a year later, in 1974, President Nixon resigned. Proof had become available that showed Nixon was involved in the Watergate Scandal. His original letter of resignation was on display at the Ford Museum for a short period of time. Ford became president at noon on August 9, 1974.

One of Ford's first decisions as president was to pardon, or excuse, Nixon for the crimes he might have committed while in office. The American people needed to focus on other issues besides Watergate. It was hurting their trust in the government. Nixon was also in poor health. Ford thought the stress of a trial could make Nixon's health worse.

Ford was president for only two years. He spent much of that time trying to rebuild the American people's faith in the government. In this photo, Chief Justice Warren Burger gives Ford the oath of office, making Ford president of the United States. Ford's wife, Betty, is shown at center.

THE PRESIDENT OVERSEAS

Ford traveled to several countries overseas. He was the first U.S. president to visit Japan. He then traveled to South Korea. There he met its president and also visited U.S. troops. Above: *Ford* (right) is shown at his final stop, the Soviet Union, where he met with President Leonid Brezhnev (left).

Ford faced several hardships. In 1975, a Cambodian ship captured an American ship, the SS *Mayaguez*, and its 39 crew members. Ford called for a military rescue. The crew and the ship were rescued, but 41 American soldiers were killed.

In 1974, Ford traveled to Vladivostok, a city in Russia, then called the Soviet Union. He met with Soviet president Leonid Brezhnev and talked generally about reducing the threat of war between the United States and the Soviet Union by limiting the number of weapons kept by each country. This meeting also led to a space mission in 1975, run by both the United States and the Soviet Union.

The Ford Museum features a large world map where museum visitors can select a location to visit. They then "travel" with President Ford to learn about the events he dealt with in the selected country.

The cold war began after World War II (1939–1945). The cold war was a struggle for power between the United States and the Soviet Union. Left: When Ford met with Brezhnev their meeting paved the way for peace and unity between the two countries. However, the cold war didn't officially end until 1989.

THE FIRST LADY

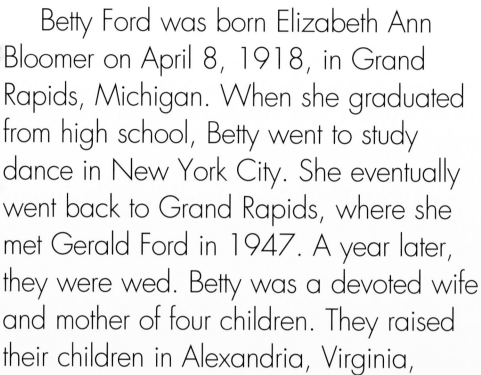

In 1978, Betty Ford became dependent on alcohol and on drugs prescribed, or given, to her by her doctor. She recovered, and in 1982, she helped to open the Betty Ford Center in Rancho Mirage, California. Today it is one of the top alcohol and drug recovery programs in the country.

Betty Ford was born Elizabeth Ann Bloomer on April 8, 1918, in Grand Rapids, Michigan. When she graduated from high school, Betty went to study dance in New York City. She eventually went back to Grand Rapids, where she met Gerald Ford in 1947. A year later, they were wed. Betty was a devoted wife and mother of four children. They raised their children in Alexandria, Virginia, before moving to the White House.

When the Ford family moved to the White House in 1974, Betty spent time working on women's health issues. At the same time, she fought and won her own battle with breast cancer, a serious, often deadly illness that affects many women.

Gerald and Betty Ford were awarded this Congressional Gold Medal (top) because of their public service to the American people. Betty Ford has been honored with at least 25 various awards since her days in the White House. These awards include the Presidential Medal of Freedom (bottom) and honors from the American Medical Association and the American Cancer Society. All of these awards are featured at the Ford Museum.

LATER YEARS

Gerald Ford has kept busy since his days in Washington, D.C. After losing the presidency to Democrat Jimmy Carter in 1976, Ford became a strong supporter for other Republicans, such as Ronald Reagan. In 2000, he wrote a *New York Times* article supporting George W. Bush's vice presidential choice, Dick Cheney.

The Fords live in Palm Springs, California. After serving in the White House, Ford became a very popular speaker and writer. For several years, he appeared at more than 200 events per year. All of Ford's writings, as well as his speeches, can be found at the Ford Library.

Above: Ford is shown accepting the John F. Kennedy Profile in Courage Award in 2001. This award was named for President John F. Kennedy. Standing to the left of Ford is Caroline Kennedy, John Kennedy's daughter, and to right is Senator Ted Kennedy, John Kennedy's brother.

Here are two magazine covers picturing Gerald Ford. He is pictured because of his political achievements. In his twenties, Ford also earned a place on the cover of a magazine. He was a fashion model and appeared on the cover of Cosmopolitan in 1942.

In 1979, Ford wrote A Time to Heal. *This is a book about his life. Most recently he wrote the introduction to A Time for Reflection: Memoirs of a Life, by Bill Simon. This book is also about Ford's life. It was published in 2001.*

DID YOU KNOW?

Here are some fun facts to share with friends about the thirty-eighth U.S. president:

Ford's favorite dessert is butter pecan ice cream, and his favorite foods are pot roast and red cabbage.

While serving in Congress, Ford was part of the group of people organized to find out who was responsible for the **assassination** of President Kennedy.

When asked how he wanted his presidential days to be remembered, Ford said, " I want to be remembered as a . . . nice person, who worked at the job, and who left the White House in better shape than when I took it over."

Ford is ambidextrous, which means he can use both hands equally well. As a child, when he was standing, he used his right hand for activities such as throwing a football. When he sat, he used his left hand to do activities such as writing.

GLOSSARY

assassination (uh-sa-sih-NAY-shun) To have killed an important person.

bribes (BRYBZ) Money or favors given in return for something else.

Congress (KON-gres) The part of the U.S. government that makes laws.

Democratic (deh-muh-KRA-tik) Referring to one of the two major political parties in the United States.

economics (eh-keh-NAH-miks) The study of production and supply and demands of goods or services.

House minority leader (HOWS my-NOR-ih-tee LEE-der) The chairperson for the party that has fewer members in the House of Representatives.

House of Representatives (HOWS UV reh-prih-ZEN-tuh-tivs) A part of Congress, the lawmaking body of the U.S. government.

National Archives and Records Administration (NA-shuh-nuhl AR-kyvz AND REH-kurdz ad-mih-nih-STRAY-shun) The group in the U.S. government that runs the 10 presidential libraries.

National Security Council (NA-shuh-nuhl sih-KYUR-ih-tee KOWN-sihl) A group of people, including the president, who meet to discuss the safety of the nation.

political science (puh-LIH-tih-kul SY-ehns) The study of government institutions and how they work.

Republican (rih-PUH-blih-kuhn) Referring to one of the two major political parties in the United States.

resigned (ree-ZYND) To have stepped down from a position.

Senate (SEN-it) A law-making part of the U.S. government.

Vietnam era (VEE-it-nahm EAR-uh) The years before and after the Vietnam War between North Vietnam and South Vietnam that the United States fought in the 1960s and early 1970s.

Watergate Scandal (WAH-tur-gayt SKAN-duhl) When members of the Republican party broke into the Democratic headquarters to steal secrets that would help President Nixon be reelected.

INDEX

PRIMARY SOURCES

Pages 5–11, 14–18, 22: Pictures were obtained from the Ford Library. **Page 19 (top):** Picture was obtained from the U.S. Mint. **Page 19 (bottom):** Picture was obtained from the John F. Kennedy Library and Museum.

WEB SITES

Due to the changing nature of Internet links, PowerKids Press has developed an online list of Web sites related to the subject of this book. This site is updated regularly. Please use this link to access the list:
www.powerkidslinks.com/pl/grflm/